What the F*@# Should I Drink?

The Answer to the Most
Important Question of Your Day
(in 75 F*@#ing Recipes)

by Zach Golden

RUNNING PRESS
PHILADELPHIA

To Mom and Dad, I'm Sorry

Running Press
Hachette Book Group
1290 Avenue of the Americas, New York, NY 10104
www.runningpress.com
@Running_Press

Printed in China
First Edition: July 2013

Published by Running Press, an imprint of Perseus Books, LLC,
a subsidiary of Hachette Book Group, Inc.

The Hachette Speakers Bureau provides a wide range of authors for speaking events. To find out more, go to www.hachettespeakersbureau.com or call (866) 376-6591.

The publisher is not responsible for websites (or their content) that are not owned by the publisher.

Print book cover and interior design by Jason Kayser.

Library of Congress Control Number: 2013931279

ISBNs: 978-0-7624-4907-1 (hardcover), 978-0-7624-5057-2 (ebook)

TLF

16   15   14   13   12   11   10   9   8

Foreword by Jesus Christ

Much has been written about my "gift" of turning water into wine. The truth is, John was an insufferable horse-fart of a human being, whose windbag fairytales got him and me into trouble more times than I care to remember. If you don't believe me, ask him about the whole "apple juice to battery acid" thing. (Christ, you futz around a preschool for one afternoon and everyone gets up in arms.) And while it's been written that the whole water to wine thing was a miracle, it's historically just a bit off.

Some back-story, if you will so indulge me. I had discovered the marvels of drink at an early age. We'll skip the Freudian bullshit (Question, doctor, how could I want to have sex with my mother if she was a notorious virgin?) and just say that being the only son of a fairly demanding father coupled with all of those fucking disciples following me, and writing down everything I said, and taking everything so fucking literally (Figs. I said I hated figs. With an "i," Goddamnit), took its toll.

It was written that we were at a wedding and blah, blah, blah, I turned water to wine. Slight embellishment, but John figured that sounded more miraculous than the two of us doing whip-its from a half-empty can of whipped cream in the shed behind his father's house, so what can you do? And I don't know where the whole "wine" thing came from—again, my assumption is that John, being a man vastly concerned with the appearance of a strong moral comportment, took some liberties with the truth. On that day I turned water into malt liquor and, several hours later, our vomit into a variety of intoxicants.

John and I spent much of our time in that shed (no homo), and soon we began experimenting with all of the spirits and mixers that I'd "miraculously" changed from other, shittier liquids. Soon, our repertoire became so vast that we would bicker about what to drink. And as things go, bickering about what to drink turned into bickering about other, more important issues. One day, amidst a vigorous debate on whether gazebos or rotundas were the superior structure, I finally had enough. I stormed out of the shed and headed back home. On the way, I ran into Judas who was acting rapier than usual, and that's considerable, given his customary rapiness is on the high side to begin with. He kissed me and I'll never forget what I said to him after that kiss: "Judas, this might be the alcohol talking, but I just want you to know, I love alcohol." Then, in one of those comedy-of-error moments that seem only to happen after a morning of heavy drinking and recreational drug use, some Jews (or Romans, I can't remember) got all Rodney King on me, blah, blah, blah, I woke up three days later. But I'm forgiving, perhaps to a fault, and here we are, so let's not dwell on it.

Divine mercy and hindsight have allowed me to since forgive John, sort of. Looking back, I realize it wasn't a matter of whether the rotunda, with its clearly superior domed roof, was better than the unfortunate gazebo. No, it was the vast plentitude of choice. With all of the libations at our disposal, choice got in the way. I look back on that day and think, if only there were a book, or a website, or a website that eventually became a book, that told us what the fuck we should drink, things would have ended differently. Or maybe they wouldn't have, who knows. I was pretty drunk most of that time.

—Jesus Christ

Run after a fake rabbit so pedophiles and miscreants can lose money with a fucking Greyhound

2 ounces vodka
¼ ounce lime juice
Grapefruit juice
Wedge of lime

If greyhound tracks served Greyhounds (the drink, you fucking psychopath) maybe they would attract a more reputable clientele, but they don't, so moot fucking point. Add the vodka and lime juice to a shaker and add some fucking ice. Shake violently until the neighbor calls 911 or for 15 seconds, whichever comes first. Strain into a rocks glass with ice, top with some fucking grapefruit juice, and garnish with a wedge of lime.

Have a fear of bus-related sex crimes? . . . . *Turn to page 55.*

Forget the
Maine after
a fucking
**Remember the
Maine**

2 ounces rye whiskey
½ ounce cherry brandy
¾ ounce sweet vermouth
Dash of absinthe
Soda water

Remember the Maine is named for the *U.S.S. Maine*, which was blown up, probably after the captain had a few too many Remember the Maines. Add the rye, cherry brandy, sweet vermouth, and absinthe to a mixing glass with plenty of fucking ice. Stir that shit proper, then strain into a chilled rocks glass and top with some fucking soda water. Then drink, and stay away from any and all nautical vessels.

Feigning seasickness
just for attention? . . . . *Turn to page 59.*

Enjoy a drink that sounds like a stripper with a fucking Brandy Alexander

1½ ounces brandy
¾ ounce crème de cacao
¾ ounce light cream
Grated nutmeg

Parents, if your child has two first names, she will end up either grinding strangers' dicks for singles, or on meth, no exceptions. Thankfully, the same isn't true for drinks. Add the brandy, crème de cacao, and cream to a shaker without ice. Shake that shit up, then add ice and fucking shake it again. Strain into a fucking cocktail glass, garnish with grated nutmeg, and serve with a healthy side of daddy issues.

You're a stripper and
this hits too close to home? . . . . . . *Turn to page 37.*

Don't kill yourself after a fucking Hemingway Daiquiri

2 ounces white rum
¾ ounce grapefruit juice
½ ounce lime juice
½ ounce Luxardo Maraschino

Hemingway could fucking drink. Sure, it drove him to an eventual suicide and all of that bad stuff, but, quick question, did you write *The Old Man and the Fucking Sea*? Oh, you didn't? Then back off. Add the white rum, grapefruit juice, lime juice, and Luxardo Maraschino to a shaker with plenty of fucking ice. Shake, strain into a cocktail glass, drink, and marvel at the fucking mustache that just adorned your face.

Trying to avoid alcoholism? . . . . . . *Turn to page 95.*

Gesticulate more with a fucking Negroni

1½ ounces gin
1½ ounces sweet vermouth
1½ ounces Campari
Orange slice

The Negroni is as Italian as fucking economic collapses, womanizing, and excessive body hair, so do enjoy. Combine the gin, sweet vermouth, and Campari in a rocks glass with some fucking ice. Stir it and add an orange slice for garnish. Then, you fucking drink it and confuse deaf people.

Have an aversion to body hair? . . . . *Turn to page 87.*

Consider building a city below sea level after a fucking Sazerac

2 ounces rye whiskey
Dash of Demerara sugar
2 dashes angostura bitters
4 dashes Peychaud's Bitters
Absinthe rinse

The Sazerac is the official cocktail of New Orleans, so stock up on beads and say hello to your old friend Regret. In an old-fashioned glass, muddle the sugar and bitters. Add the fucking rye whiskey and some ice, and stir that shit up. Rinse another old-fashioned glass with absinthe and strain the delicious alcoholy contents from the other fucking glass into the absinthe-rinsed one. Fucking drink it and ignore any and all mandatory evacuations.

Looking for less widespread destruction? . . . . *Turn to page 43.*

Wish women couldn't vote with a fucking **Old Fashioned**

2 ounces rye whiskey
Dash of Demerara sugar
Dash of orange bitters
Dash of old-fashioned bitters
Orange twist

Despite this being one of the greatest drinks in the world, nostalgia is quite confusing. Sure, "back then" people were more polite and you didn't have to lock your front door, but "back then" people still died of polio and the internet was slow as fuck. In a rocks glass, muddle the sugar with the fucking bitters. Add some ice and the rye whiskey, and stir until cold. Add a twist of orange, put on some Dean Martin, and wonder why cats used to wear pajamas.

Don't feel like talking about your five-mile walk to school in the snow that was uphill both ways? .... *Turn to page 79.*

Complete your cougar costume with a fucking Cosmopolitan

2 ounces vodka
¼ ounce Cointreau
¼ ounce lime juice
½ ounce cranberry juice

The Cosmopolitan rose to fame when four vapid characters from a television show about sex within a particular city found it was a tastier alternative to ejaculate. Pour the vodka, Cointreau, lime juice, and cranberry juice into a shaker and add ice. Shake that shit up like a baby that won't stop crying, and strain into a cocktail glass. Drink until the tears stop.

Don't want to die alone? . . . . *Turn to page 145.*

Drive worse after a fucking Sidecar

2 ounces cognac
1 ounce Cointreau
¾ ounce lemon juice

When most people hear "sidecar," they picture a cartoon dog with leather goggles on the side of a motorcycle, but now that you've got this fucking book, you're smarter than that, aren't you? Pour the cognac, Cointreau, and lemon juice into a shaker and add ice. Shake it up, strain into a chilled cocktail glass, and hide your keys.

Don't want to abandon your leather goggles? . . . . *Turn to page 113.*

Play some circus music and reminisce upon your first time with a fucking Margarita

2 ounces tequila blanco
1 ounce Cointreau
¾ ounce lime juice

Margaritas are the water that makes the "I just cheated on my spouse" plant grow strong, so be careful. Add the tequila blanco, Cointreau, and lime juice to a shaker and add some fucking ice. Shake and strain into a margarita glass, with salted rim, much like pants, totally optional.

Uncomfortable with Spanish-sounding words? . . . . *Turn to page 7.*

Find your Lucky Pierre with a fucking French 75

1½ ounces dry gin
1 teaspoon superfine sugar
½ ounce lemon juice
Champagne

We can thank the French for many things: French fries, French dip sandwiches, and the Lucky Pierre. Now, we can also add the fucking French 75 to the illustrious list. Add the gin, sugar, and lemon juice to a shaker and add some fucking ice. Shake that shit. Strain into a champagne flute and top with Champagne, or whatever cheap fucking alternative you will probably be using. *Sacré bleu*, fucking enjoy.

Chain-smoking and being short not your thing? . . . . *Turn to page 27.*

Fondle yourself next to an upscale cat yoga studio after a fucking Manhattan

2 ounces rye whiskey
1 ounce sweet vermouth
2 dashes angostura bitters

Ah, Manhattan. Not just the most expensive place in the country, but also one of the few remaining places you can still see a real-live hobo orgy. And, it's a delightful fucking drink. Add the rye whiskey, vermouth, and bitters to a rocks glass with some fucking ice. Strain into a chilled cocktail glass and charge your friends way too much money for it.

Haven't acquired a taste
for widespread filth? . . . . *Turn to page 99.*

Embarrass your family with a fucking Rusty Nail

1½ ounces Scotch
½ ounce Drambuie
Lemon twist

This drink, plain and simple, will make your insides feel like you're carrying the devil's illegitimate chud baby. Add the Scotch and Drambuie to a rocks glass filled with ice. Stir gently and garnish with a fucking twist of lemon. Drink and start drafting apology texts.

Already suffering from one too many blood-borne diseases? . . . . *Turn to page 131.*

Don't get the girl with a fucking Martini

2¾ ounces gin
¼ ounce dry vermouth
Olive

"**T**he name is Kleinberg, Mort Kleinberg." If you're not 007, don't fucking try it. But by all means, try this. Pour the gin and dry vermouth into a mixing glass with plenty of fucking ice. Stir well and strain into a fancy martini glass and garnish with an olive.

Don't feel like throwing up in a taxi? . . . . *Turn to page 71.*

Consider a Pacific Rim job after mastering a fucking Mai Tai

2 ounces dark rum
½ ounce orgeat syrup
½ ounce orange curaçao
1 ounce lime juice

Tiki bars are as important an American tradition as morbid obesity, so fly your flag high while making the beloved Mai Tai. Add the fucking dark rum, orgeat syrup, orange curaçao, and lime juice to a shaker and add some fucking ice. Shake and strain into a rocks glass with ice. Garnish with a fucking tiki head or a pineapple or some shit.

Still call Asian people Orientals? . . . . Turn to page 123.

Understand its name the next morning with a fucking Dark 'N' Stormy

2 ounces spiced rum
  (Gosling's recommended)
¾ ounce lime juice
Ginger beer

Hide your fucking keys, unless you love drunk driving, in which case put them somewhere readily accessible, because this shit is delicious and will fuck you up. Add the spiced rum and lime juice to a shaker and add ice. Shake that shit up and strain into a highball glass with plenty of fucking ice. Top it all with some fucking ginger beer, drink too many, and ask yourself whether your pants are wet from the ocean or from your urine.

Need to function productively
in the next couple of days? . . . . *Turn to page 105.*

Be thankful you're nowhere near Kentucky with a fucking Mint Julep

2 ounces bourbon
6 mint leaves
2 sugar cubes
Dash of angostura bitters

Most people think that the only time a Mint Julep is appropriate is when tiny men ride a fucking horse really fast as people watch in stupid hats, but, plain and simple, those people are fucking wrong. In a mixing glass, muddle the fucking mint and sugar until they have spiritually and literally become one. Add a bunch of crushed ice, the bourbon, and the bitters, and fucking stir that shit up. Strain and serve in one of those insufferable mint julep glasses and make everyone hate you just a little bit more.

It's not Derby Day? . . . . *Turn to page 67.*

Trick a Mormon into drinking with a fucking Mojito

2 ounces white rum
8 mint leaves
¾ ounce lime juice
½ ounce simple syrup
1 teaspoon granulated sugar
Soda water

Mojitos are the perfect drink for tricking your dumb friend who doesn't drink into drinking: They're sweet and acidic, and generally result in impromptu games of "just the tip." Muddle the mint, lime, and sugar until unfucked up. Add ice, the rum, and the simple syrup, then fucking top that shit with soda water. Garnish with a mint sprig and some lime and drink until you assume another type of missionary position.

Want a drink that doesn't end in crying? .... *Turn to page 95.*

Reveal your lack of worldliness while pronouncing Caipirinha

2 ounces cachaça
¾ ounce lime juice
2 lime wedges
½ ounce simple syrup
1 teaspoon granulated sugar

The Caipirinha is the official fucking drink of Brazil, so while drinking expect a fine mix of beautiful women, sandy beaches, and random gunfire. In a shaker, muddle the lime wedges and sugar until they're ready to fucking listen. Then add some crushed ice, the cachaça, lime juice, and simple syrup, and shake. Strain into a rocks glass with ice, drink it, and make a well-timed hairless asshole joke.

Averse to hair removal? . . . . *Turn to page 139.*

Finally try bath salts after drinking a fucking Zombie

½ ounce white rum
1 ounce gold rum
½ ounce dark rum
1 ounce lime juice
Splash of pineapple juice

It's not called a Zombie because it's a popular fucking drink on yachts. It's called a Zombie because a few too many will get you pants-shittingly drunk. Add all of the fucking ingredients to a shaker with ice. Set aside the craving for brains and fucking shake, then strain into a highball glass filled with ice and commence forgetting your name.

Allergic to awesome? . . . . *Turn to page 152.*

Match your beverage's fruitiness with a fucking Classic Daiquiri

2 ounces white rum
¾ ounce lime juice
¾ ounce simple syrup

You may know the Classic Daiquiri from its second cousin once removed, the Frozen Daiquiri. But unlike its frozen kin, the Classic Daiquiri doesn't taste of body shots and herpes, so fucking have at it. Add the white rum, lime juice, and simple syrup to a shaker with some fucking ice and fucking shake it. Strain into a chilled cocktail glass and fucking drink that shit.

Big fan of Don't Ask,
Don't Tell? . . . . *Turn to page 11.*

Demand forcefully that you're not argumentative with a fucking Last Word

¾ ounce Green Chartreuse
¾ ounce London dry gin
¾ ounce lime juice
¾ ounce Luxardo Maraschino

This is a fucking prohibition-era cocktail developed at the Detroit Athletic Club by a bartender named Robocop, so you know it's good. Add the Green Chartreuse, gin, lime juice, and Luxardo Maraschino to a shaker with some fucking ice. Shake that shit like you mean business and strain into a chilled cocktail glass. Then drink it and fucking cut people off mid-sentence.

Need to get the penultimate word in? . . . . *Turn to page 117.*

Feel worse tomorrow with a fucking Ramos Gin Fizz

2 ounces gin
½ ounce cream
1 egg white
Dash of lemon juice

This shit's got raw egg and cream in it. Sounds fucking gross, right? Wrong, asshole, it's fucking delicious. God, don't you get sick of being wrong all the time? Add the gin, cream, egg white, and lemon juice to a shaker with no fucking ice, none of it. Shake that shit up, then add ice to the shaker, and shake again. Shake a bit fucking longer, approximately the length of time a baby sea otter takes to nap, divided by four, plus Bon Jovi. Strain into a highball glass and fucking drink.

Don't like drinks with omelet ingredients? . . . . *Turn to page 19.*

Finally remember to cancel AOL with a fucking 20th Century

½ ounce London dry gin
¾ ounce lemon juice
¾ ounce crème de cacao
¾ ounce Lillet Blanc

The 20th Century wasn't that great. Sure, some technological progress was made and the end of the world was averted on a few occasions, but I counter all of that with JNCO jeans. Thankfully, this drink is better than the century. Add the gin, lemon juice, crème de cacao, and Lillet Blanc to a shaker with a bunch of fucking ice. Shake and strain into a cocktail glass. Drink and thank God it's the 21st century as you expose your messy genitals on Chatroulette.

You're Amish and swear off anything after the 18th century? . . . . *Turn to page 91.*

Convince every 16-year-old girl at the party it's totally not weird with a fucking Lemon Drop

2 ounces vodka
¾ ounce lemon juice
¾ ounce simple syrup

The Lemon Drop is the martini's gay cousin, not that there's anything wrong with that and shit. Add the vodka, lemon juice, and simple syrup to a shaker with some fucking ice and shake. Strain into a fucking cocktail glass, and brush up on your statutory rape laws.

Chemically castrated? . . . . *Turn to page 127.*

Become clairvoyant and see diarrhea in your future with a fucking Diamondback

1½ ounces rye whiskey
¾ ounce Green Chartreuse
¾ ounce apple brandy

This isn't one of those "sip on the porch while you enjoy the sunset" drinks. Fuck no, it's a "let's start a cockfighting ring in space" type of drink. Add the rye whiskey, Green Chartreuse, and apple brandy to a shaker with some fucking ice. Shake that shit up, and strain into a chilled cocktail glass. Fucking drink it and explain to your pantsless friend that cockfighting is with roosters.

Not in the mood to black out? . . . . *Turn to page 9.*

Deem your toilet and mattress interchangeable with a fucking Rob Roy

1½ ounces Scotch
½ ounce sweet vermouth
2 dashes angostura bitters

People with two first names should be sent back in time so they can slap their parents for fucking up the rest of their lives. Rob Roy, however, is an exception, since he has a delicious drink named after him. Add the Scotch, sweet vermouth, and bitters to a mixing glass filled with ice. Fucking stir that shit up, then strain into a chilled cocktail glass. Drink that shit and wish you had a drink named after you, rather than a child safety statute.

Not a fan of old man drinks? . . . . *Turn to page 80.*

Have less scurvy with a fucking Gimlet

2 ounces London dry gin
¾ ounce lime juice
¾ ounce simple syrup

The gimlet was introduced by the British Royal Navy to fight scurvy, which may explain the track record of the British Royal Navy. Add the fucking gin, lime juice, and simple syrup to a shaker with ice. Shake that fucker up, and strain into a cocktail glass. Drink a few, and ward off any and all pirate-related diseases.

Want more scurvy? . . . . *Turn to page 135.*

Enlarge your liver with a fucking Gibson

2¾ ounces London dry gin
¼ ounce dry vermouth
Cocktail onions

There's a lot of uncertainty as to where the fuck this cocktail got its name, so we'll just make shit up. A pre-post-op transvestite named Barry got his/future-her heart broken by a convincing scarecrow named Winston, but the bartender, whose hearing hadn't been the same since the goldfish accident, heard Gibson, and *voilà*. Add the gin and dry vermouth to a mixing glass with a shitload of ice. Stir that shit up like an abortion joke at church, and strain into a chilled cocktail glass. Garnish with cocktail onions and fucking imbibe.

Want to make worse decisions? . . . . *Turn to page 23.*

Don't say "bomb" while drinking a fucking Aviation

2 ounces gin
¾ ounce Luxardo Maraschino
¾ ounce lemon juice
Dash of crème de violette

Drinking on the plane, or while flying it, is fun as shit, so it makes sense that there's a cocktail named after it. Add the gin, Luxardo Maraschino, lemon juice, and crème de violette to a shaker with a bunch of fucking ice. Shake violently while humming Ziggy Stardust, strain into a cocktail glass, and please return your seat backs to their upright positions.

Still skeptical that oxygen is flowing even when the bag doesn't inflate? . . . . *Turn to page 31.*

Have cocktail drink you with a fucking **Moscow Mule**

2 ounces vodka
¾ ounce lime juice
Ginger beer

Russians can fucking drink. You would too, if all of your men looked like Bond villains and it was balls-tighteningly cold all the time, so any drink named after them must be fucking serious. Add the vodka and lime juice to a shaker with some fucking ice, and shake that shit up. Strain into a copper cup with ice (which of course you don't fucking own, so grudgingly, a rocks glass will suffice), and top with ginger beer.

Not a fan of vomit? . . . . *Turn to page 85.*

Drink something named after where you'll be urinating with a fucking **Between the Sheets**

1 ounce cognac
1 ounce white rum
¾ ounce Cointreau
½ ounce lemon juice
½ ounce Bénédictine D.O.M

I t's funny how all of the cocktails with allusions to sex never result in any. And not "ha-ha" funny, more "cat lady funny" or "you're taking your blow-up doll on vacation" funny. Add all of the fucking ingredients to a shaker with plenty of ice and shake. Strain into a chilled cocktail glass, and cheers to your continued loneliness.

Allergic to cat ladies? . . . . *Turn to page 149.*

Recollect your bout of Chlamydia with a fucking Stinger

2½ ounces brandy
½ ounce crème de menthe

The stinger has been called a whore's drink, which must preclude semen from being considered a beverage. Add the brandy and crème de menthe to a fucking shaker with some ice. Shake and strain into a chilled cocktail glass and, just like when you got that promotion, down the hatch.

Not a whore? . . . . *Turn to page 45.*

Don't fuck up a fucking Jack Rose

2 ounces apple brandy
¾ ounce grenadine
¾ ounce lemon juice

T he Jack Rose is a classic fucking cocktail. Hell,
Hemingway wrote about it, so don't go and fuck it
up or I'll get you with a knife. Add the apple brandy,
grenadine, and lemon juice to a shaker with some ice.
Fucking shake until you don't think you can shake
anymore, about 15 seconds, you fucking weakling.
Strain into a chilled cocktail glass and celebrate your
ability to not ruin everything.

**Drinking a man's name
makes you uncomfortable?** . . . . . *Turn to page 137.*

Sound like a drunk grandmother with a fucking Bee's Knees

2 ounces gin
¾ ounce lemon juice
½ ounce honey
Lemon twist

I fucking hate bees. When they almost mysteriously went extinct, well, I won't give too much away but, you're welcome. The Bee's Knees makes me hate bees marginally less, but they still fucking suck. (Bees that is. This drink is fucking awesome.) Combine all of that shit into a shaker with some ice. Fucking shake, strain into a chilled glass, and garnish with a dead hornet, or a twist of lemon.

One of those creepy
urban beekeepers? . . . . *Turn to page 101.*

Find our next president outside Home Depot with a fucking El Presidente

1½ ounces white rum
½ ounce orange curaçao
¾ ounce Dolin Blanc vermouth
Dash of grenadine

The Cubans have given us many great things: cigars, amazing baseball players, and crime. Now, we can fucking add this drink to that list. Add all that fucking shit to a mixing glass with plenty of fucking ice. Stir it up, then strain into a chilled cocktail glass. Put on a wifebeater, play some fucking dominoes, and drink.

Dutifully observing a trade embargo? . . . . *Turn to page 13.*

Wonder if masturbation counts as sex with a fucking **Sex on the Beach**

2 ounces vodka
½ ounce peach Schnapps
Cranberry juice
Orange juice

Sex on the beach is vastly overrated. There's nothing romantic about sand in your babymaking extremities, and the smell of fish really isn't an aphrodisiac. So while fucking on the beach isn't that great, this drink fucking is. Add the vodka and peach Schnapps to a shaker with ice and shake the fucking shit out of it. Strain into a highball glass with plenty of fucking ice, and top with equal parts cranberry juice and orange juice. Garnish with disappointment.

Angry at your liver? . . . . *Turn to page 51.*

Loot your city after a fucking Hurricane

1 ounce light rum
1 ounce dark rum
½ ounce lime juice
1 teaspoon passion fruit juice

Hurricanes, much like their meteorological counterparts, result in families fucking torn apart, utter devastation, and public nudity, so careful, Sport. Add the light rum, dark rum, lime juice, and passion fruit juice to a shaker with some fucking ice. Shake that shit up, and strain into the cheapest plastic cup you find, filled with ice. Drink and tell people you love them, no, you fucking lovvvvve them, man.

Don't feel like evacuating? . . . . . *Turn to page 111.*

Eventually throw up a fucking
Sea Breeze

2 ounces vodka
¾ ounce grapefruit juice
Cranberry juice

I've got a problem with girly drinks. And not with the fucking drinks, but with the designation of them as "girly." Just because something's pink means it's girly? It's not our fault that cranberry juice turns shit pink, and that sometimes making out with dudes is way more convenient. Add the vodka and grapefruit juice to a shaker with some fucking ice. Shake and strain into a highball glass filled with ice, then top with some fucking cranberry juice and hold with a slightly limp wrist.

Your father's not accepting? . . . . . *Turn to page 49.*

Be more insufferable with a fucking Greenpoint

2 ounces rye whiskey
½ ounce Yellow Chartreuse
½ ounce sweet vermouth
Dash of angostura bitters
Dash of orange bitters

Ah, Greenpoint, home to hardworking Polish immigrants, and mustachioed twenty-somethings whose interests include irony, things you don't know about yet, and sodomy. Add all that fucking shit to a mixing glass with ice. Give it a good fucking stir, then strain into a cocktail glass. Drink and claim that you liked this cocktail way before it was cool.

Never ridden the G-Train? . . . . . . *Turn to page 121.*

Keep insisting that Iranian and Persian are different with a fucking Jasmine

1½ ounces gin
¾ ounce Campari
¾ ounce lemon juice
1 ounce Cointreau

Gin isn't just for old white British women, you racist asshole. Especially in the Jasmine, which no self-respecting WASP would touch with a croquet mallet. Add the gin, Campari, lemon juice, and Cointreau to a shaker with a shitload of ice and, shocker, shake it. Strain into a cocktail glass, and fucking drink with your pinkies out.

Afraid of Aladdin jokes? . . . . *Turn to page 63.*

Be more stereotypically Irish by drinking too many fucking John Collins

2 ounces bourbon
1 ounce lemon juice
¾ ounce simple syrup
Soda water

J ohn Collins is Tom Collins's brother who has a taste for bourbon, is a little classier, and once dated a stripper named Marmalade. Add the bourbon, lemon juice, and simple syrup to a fucking shaker with some ice. Shake that shit up, strain into a Collins glass, and top that motherfucker off with some soda water. Then fucking drink, call your brother that you'll never live up to, breathe loudly into the phone, hang up, and repeat.

Don't house an intolerable hatred for Protestants? . . . . *Turn to page 133.*

Make things not worse, for once, with a fucking Kir Royale

3 ounces Champagne
½ ounce cassis

This is the easiest fucking recipe in this book, and perhaps the world. On a scale of one to easy, it's your little sister. Pour a fucking glass of Champagne. Add the fucking cassis, stir that shit up, and bask in the warm glow of easiness.

Have nothing to celebrate? . . . . . . *Turn to page 21.*

Feel less horrible after a fucking Corpse Reviver #2

¾ ounce gin
¾ ounce lemon juice
¾ ounce Cointreau
¾ ounce Lillet Blanc
2 dashes absinthe

The Corpse Reviver #2 is a traditional fucking "hair of the dog" hangover cure. While on the subject, other cures include smoking weed, sleeping, and burying Asian hookers. Combine all of that shit in a fucking shaker with ice. Shake until the dead awaken, roughly 15 seconds, and strain into a chilled glass. Drink, and feel less horrible.

Not currently dry-heaving? . . . . . . *Turn to page 15.*

Use the term "food politics" while drinking a fucking Brooklyn Folly

2 ounces Scotch
¾ ounce dry vermouth
½ ounce Cynar
½ ounce St. Germain
Dash of Peychaud's Bitters

B rooklyn is one of the most confusing fucking places in the world. On one hand, there are good people who've been there for ages, and on the other hand, there is Park Slope, where gender-neutral yuppies raise kids I hate. But it's fucking home, so what can you do? Drink, that's what. Add the Scotch, vermouth, Cynar, St. Germain, and bitters to a mixing glass with plenty of fucking ice. Strain into a chilled cocktail glass and pour with irony, then tell a fucking food blogger to stop taking photos.

Not a yuppie? . . . . *Turn to page 81.*

Speak worse French with a fucking Champs Élysées

2 ounces cognac
¾ ounce lemon juice
½ ounce Yellow Chartreuse
¼ ounce simple syrup
Dash of angostura bitters

The Champs Élysées is named after the fanny-pack haven in Paris because riders in the fucking Tour de France drink this on the final leg while humming "America the Beautiful" in French. None of that is true, but it's printed in a fucking book, so who are you to argue? Add the cognac, lemon juice, Yellow Chartreuse, simple syrup, and bitters to a fucking ice-filled shaker. Shake that shit up, strain into a cocktail glass, and *à fucking santé*.

Wish French were a dead language? . . . . *Turn to page 47.*

Be thankful you're not Criss Angel with a fucking Archangel

2¼ ounces gin
¾ ounce Aperol
2 cucumber slices
Lemon twist

I would address Criss Angel fans here, but because they don't fucking exist, we can all just agree that that guy is a living Ed Hardy shirt. In a fucking mixing glass, muddle a slice of cucumber, then add the fucking gin, Aperol, and some fucking ice. Stir, strain into a chilled cocktail glass, and garnish with another slice of cucumber and a lemon twist. Drink, and attempt to levitate into a ceiling fan.

You are Criss Angel? . . . . *Turn to page 125.*

Reminisce upon losing your virginity on the beach with a fucking Blood and Sand

¾ ounce Scotch
¾ ounce orange juice
¾ ounce Cherry Heering
¾ ounce sweet vermouth

If you had a time machine, and could go back to prom night, and you were awesome, you'd make this instead of throwing up Red Bull and vodkas all night. It wouldn't change the tear-filled sex romp, but at least the drinks would be good. Add the Scotch, orange juice, Cheery Heering, and vermouth to a cocktail shaker with a fucking shitload of ice. Shake and strain into a cocktail glass. Drink until it stops hurting, emotionally.

Don't want to be confused for having a vagina? . . . . *Turn to page 17.*

Be more like the French with a fucking Bitter French

1 ounce gin
½ ounce lemon juice
¼ ounce Campari
½ ounce simple syrup
Champagne

It's very en vogue to hate the French, what with their criticism of fucking foreign policy, slight air of pretension, and preference for anal sex. But the French gave us a fucking abundance of food and drink, as well as people to make fun of, so win-win. Add the gin, lemon juice, Campari, and simple syrup to a cocktail shaker with ice. Fucking shake it up, and strain into a champagne flute, which is the only thing less masculine than the musical instrument flute, and top with some, you fucking guessed it, Champagne.

Run out of French jokes? . . . . *Turn to page 89.*

Don't forget to renew your gang membership with a fucking Southside

2 ounces gin
1 ounce lime juice
¾ ounce simple syrup
5 mint leaves

The Southside is the Mojito's waspy cousin whose only affiliation with Cuban people is the guy who cleans the pool. In a shaker, muddle the fucking mint leaves with the lime juice and simple syrup. Add the gin and ice and fucking shake that shit like a baby holding a Polaroid picture. Strain into a chilled cocktail glass, garnish with mint leaves, and go drive by those fucking Northsiders.

You're not old and white and thus hate gin? . . . . *Turn to page 25.*

Inbreed with a fucking Queen's Road

1½ ounces aged rum
½ ounce orange juice
½ ounce lime juice
¼ ounce honey
Ginger beer

M onarchy is confusing, more so than metaphysics, convincing shemales, or foreplay. Since I don't know much about the queen, I'll assume her road is winding and littered with many a crashed car, given the drink of its namesake. Add the aged rum, orange juice, lime juice, and honey to a fucking shaker with ice. Shake like from a mixture of elation and inbreeding, strain into a Collins glass and top with some fucking ginger beer, then take that stupid fucking tiara off your head right this minute.

Want to be a better alcoholic? . . . . *Turn to page 151.*

Turn your drinking problem into a solution with a fucking Rattlesnake

2 ounces rye whiskey
¾ ounce lemon juice
¾ ounce simple syrup
2 dashes absinthe
Dash of angostura bitters
1 egg white

Rattlesnakes are the big fat pussy of the snake world. Sure, venom and shit, but they've got a fucking rattle. That's like a serial killer who wears flip-flops: boogedy, boogedy, boogedy. Fortunately for this shithole snake species, it's got a fucking delicious drink named after it. Add the fucking rye, lemon juice, simple syrup, absinthe, bitters, and egg white to a fucking shaker without ice. No fucking ice, no fucking problem. Shake, then add ice, then shake again. Strain into a cocktail glass, drink, and fucking repeat.

Had a traumatic childhood snake experience? . . . . *Turn to page 61.*

Breastfeed in public while drinking a fucking Honeysuckle

2 ounces white rum
¾ ounce lime juice
¾ ounce honey

There's a group of people who don't like honey. They're called assholes. Honey makes this drink not suck, while assholes just have shit come out of them and occasionally other accoutrements go in, so you choose which you'd like to associate with. Add the white rum, lime juice, and honey to a shaker of ice. Shake, strain into a cocktail glass, and don't be an asshole.

Don't have tits? . . . . *Turn to page 129.*

Be less not drunk with a fucking Gin Mule

2 ounces gin
¾ ounce lime juice
½ ounce simple syrup
6 mint leaves
Ginger beer

The Gin Mule is a second cousin to the fucking Moscow Mule, only it's classier, mintier, and doesn't try to sell its women for green cards. In a shaker, muddle the mint, lime juice, and simple syrup. Add the gin and some fucking ice, and shake. Strain into a highball glass filled with ice, top with ginger beer, and get fancy as fuck by garnishing with mint leaves.

Need to operate heavy machinery in the near future? . . . . *Turn to page 53.*

Declare war on sobriety with a fucking Vieux Carré

1 ounce rye whiskey
1 ounce cognac
½ ounce sweet vermouth
¼ ounce Bénédictine D.O.M
Dash of Peychaud's Bitters
Dash of angostura bitters
Lemon twist

The Vieux Carré was invented in a bar in New Orleans that is a working, revolving fucking carousel. If that doesn't sound like statutory rape bait, I don't know what does. In a fucking double rocks glass filled with ice, add the rye, cognac, vermouth, Bénédictine D.O.M, and bitters. Stir that shit up, garnish with a fucking twist of lemon, and familiarize yourself with your state's age of consent.

Sounds fucking disgusting? . . . . *Turn to page 141.*

Have something most Italians don't with a fucking Italian Job

2 ounces gin
¾ ounce grapefruit juice
½ ounce Aperol
¼ ounce Campari
Soda water

I taly's economy is a fucking disaster. The only
industry on the rise is underage prostitution and, now
that Silvio Berlusconi is no longer prime minister,
that, too, is in shambles. Thankfully, they've got some
fucking awesome drinks. Add the gin, grapefruit juice,
Aperol, and Campari to a fucking shaker filled with
ice. Shake, bitch. Strain into a highball glass filled with
ice, and top with the fucking buzzkill of the beverage
world, soda water.

**Want to simulate
time travel?** . . . . *Turn to page 83.*

Explain that over there, it's perfectly legal with a fucking Holland Gin Cocktail

2 ounces Bols Genever gin
½ ounce Luxardo Maraschino
¼ ounce simple syrup
2 dashes Peychaud's Bitters
Lemon twist

Holland is probably best known for the city of
Amsterdam. And Amsterdam is definitely best
known for hookers and tourists in tie-dye walking around
like assholes because it's legal to smoke weed. That
being said, there are no hookers or marijuana in this
fucking drink. Add the gin, Luxardo Maraschino, simple
syrup, and bitters to a fucking mixing glass filled with ice.
Stir that shit and strain into a cocktail glass. Garnish
with a lemon twist, drink, and fucking debate the
merits of wooden shoes.

Clogs slowing you down? . . . . . . *Turn to page 147.*

Wash down the body of Christ with a fucking Presbyterian

2 ounces bourbon
½ ounce lime juice
Ginger beer
Soda water

Christ could purportedly turn water to wine, to which I say, big fucking deal. Now if he could turn water to a fucking Presbyterian, well then, I'm listening. Add the fucking bourbon and lime juice to a shaker filled with ice and fucking shake. Strain into a highball glass with a fuckload of ice, and top with equal parts ginger beer and soda water. Drink, and become the patron saint of affordable turtlenecks.

Scared of eternal damnation? . . . . *Turn to page 57.*

Reenact the Jonestown Massacre with a fucking

Gin Daisy

1½ ounces gin
¾ ounce lemon juice
½ ounce Cointreau
¼ ounce simple syrup
Soda water

If I were a cult leader, I wouldn't put death juice in fucking Kool-Aid, I'd put it in a fucking Gin Daisy so my followers could get their buzz on before they got all, you know, dead. Add the gin, lemon juice, Cointreau, and simple syrup to a shaker with some fucking ice. Shake that shit up, and strain into a rocks glass. Top with soda water, have a friend try a sip, and if they don't die after five minutes, fucking drink.

Want to remember your name? . . . . *Turn to page 93.*

wonder what
constitutes
heavy
machinery
with a fucking
Martinez

1½ ounces Old Tom Gin
1½ ounces sweet vermouth
¼ ounce or a dash of maraschino liqueur
2 dashes Peychaud's Bitters

The Martinez is a fucking predecessor to the martini, even though it sounds like it's the martini's gardener. But it's not, you fucking racist. Add all that shit to a mixing glass filled with ice, and stir until everything's cold as fuck. Strain into a chilled cocktail glass, perform the Mexican Hat Dance, and fucking enjoy.

Convinced our border needs a wall? . . . . *Turn to page 65.*

Outsource capital punishment with a fucking Mexican Firing Squad

2 ounces tequila blanco
¾ ounce lime juice
¾ ounce grenadine
2 dashes orange bitters
Soda water

T he Mexican Firing Squad is a delicious fucking drink,
and also what I called my family's assholes when
we vacationed in Cancún and drank the water. Add
everyfuckingthing to a shaker with plenty of ice. Shake
that shit and strain into a highball glass filled with ice.
Top with some fucking soda water and locate the nearest
bathroom, immediately. Seriously, do it now.

Afraid to drink something with
"Mexican" in the name? . . . . *Turn to page 143.*

Place an embargo on sobriety with a fucking
Old Cuban

1½ ounces white rum
¾ ounce lime juice
¾ ounce simple syrup
6 mint leaves
Sparkling wine

An Old Cuban is like a grown-up fucking Mojito. While Mojito is running around playing grab-ass and smoking marijuana cigarettes, the Old Cuban is staying classy and civilized. Also, it's building life rafts, because that's what Cubans do. In a fucking shaker, muddle the mint leaves, simple syrup, and lime juice. Then, add the booze and a plentitude of ice, and shake that shit up. Strain into a chilled cocktail glass, top with some fucking sparkling wine, and fucking drink that shit, Papi.

Get seasick on life rafts? . . . . *Turn to page 29.*

Enjoy honorable taste elation for your inside body with a fucking Japanese Cocktail

2 ounces cognac
½ ounce orgeat syrup
½ teaspoon lemon juice
4 dashes angostura bitters
2 dashes Peychaud's Bitters

For enjoyment optimal fabrication, put all fucking ingredients into shaker impregnated with so much very ice. Violently hand shake and strain into one chilled a cocktail glass. Fucking enjoy, please thank you.

Not of enjoyment time for you, thirst haver? . . . . *Turn to page 77.*

Pretend you're a very convincing post-op transvestite with a fucking Dark Horse

2 ounces Campari
¾ ounce dry gin
Soda water
Orange peel

The Dark Horse is considered a drink for women. And men, I know what you're thinking: "It's cool, bro, I'm so secure with my sexuality that I can order a Dark Horse and it'd be no big deal." Aw, you're so cute when you're so totally, completely fucking wrong. Add the Campari and gin to a fucking highball glass with plenty of ice, and stir that shit up proper. Top with soda water, garnish with some fucking orange peel, and remember, if you're sipping this, I consider you a lady.

Don't want a girly drink? . . . . *Turn to page 107.*

Turn splotchy red and pass out after a single fucking Samurai

1½ ounces vodka
¾ ounce Cointreau
¾ ounce lemon juice

If ninja movies have taught us anything, it's that Asians can't handle their liquor. That being said, this drink will knock any samurai on his or her ass—any samurai except Steven Seagal (because he's white). Add everything to a fucking shaker filled with ice. Shake the fuck out of it like it's nunchucks or something, then strain into a chilled cocktail glass. Then consider growing a ponytail and fighting crime in Tokyo.

Too fat to fit into ninja gear? . . . . . *Turn to page 33.*

Get a call out of the blue asking to borrow money with a fucking Old Pal

1 ounce Campari
1 ounce dry vermouth
1 ounce rye whiskey
Orange twist

When I hear "old pal," I tend to think it's a euphemism for a cold sore, but in this case and very few others, I'd be wrong. Add the Campari, vermouth, and whiskey to a mixing glass with some fucking ice. Stir that shit up until cold as fuck, and strain into a chilled cocktail glass. Garnish that shit with a fucking orange twist and now that you think about it maybe it's time to refill your Valtrex prescription, you know, "just in case."

Not a burgeoning alcoholic? . . . . . *Turn to page 97.*

Drive faster with a fucking Monte Carlo

2 ounces rye whiskey
¾ ounce Bénédictine D.O.M
Dash of angostura bitters

U nless you're an Iraqi oil magnate, a Bond film villain, or inbred royalty, you would probably not have too much fun in Monte Carlo. Getting down with a few of the drink named after it, however, is a different fucking story. Add all of the fucking ingredients to a mixing glass with a shitload of ice. Stir until cold as fuck, then strain into a chilled cocktail glass. Enjoy and talk with an indiscernible accent and a certain *je ne sais quoi* that only you know is really advanced syphilis.

Driver's license revoked? . . . . *Turn to page 35.*

Declare a crusade on sobriety with a fucking Fallen Angel

1½ ounces gin
¾ ounce lemon juice
¼ ounce crème de menthe
Dash of angostura bitters

Any drink whose name alludes to both falling out of favor with God and death is sure to fuck you up, though this one could refer to an obese Mexican man who tripped. Who knows? Add the gin, lemon juice, crème de menthe, and bitters to a fucking shaker with a shitload of ice. Shake the proper amount of time to not fuck things up, about 15 seconds. Strain into a chilled cocktail glass and lament over how much better you'd look with a halo.

Want to get pants-shittingly drunk? .... Turn to page 103.

Take an exotic mouth vacation with a fucking Barbary Coast

¼ ounce white rum
¼ ounce dry gin
½ ounce Scotch
½ ounce crème de cacao
½ ounce cream

Scotch and gin in the same cocktail sounds about as appetizing as your mother and father having one of their night wrestles, but thankfully the Barbary Coast is significantly less traumatizing. Add all of that shit to a shaker with no ice. You fucking got that? No ice, you big asshole. Shake it vigorously, make a jack-off joke, then add ice and shake again. No complaining. Strain into a highball glass with plenty of ice and tell your mouth, "You're welcome."

Need to forget your childhood? . . . . *Turn to page 64.*

Tell a stranger you love them after a fucking Holt 45

Recipe by Yujin Lee

2 ounces vodka
½ ounce lemon juice
Dash of Demerara sugar
4 sprigs basil
2 cucumber slices

Herbs in cocktails seem to have gotten popular around the same time the word "mixologist" became an acceptable label for every fucking struggling actor and coke-addicted high school dropout who tends bar at places named after various venereal diseases. While "mixologist" is still the worst, herbs are fucking great—like basil, for example. In a fucking shaker, muddle the sugar, basil, and cucumber with the lemon juice. Add vodka and ice and shake. Strain into a chilled cocktail glass and figure out a sham name for your occupation.

Hate things that are wonderful? . . . . *Turn to page 109.*

Pronounce your own name incorrectly with a fucking Andrade

Recipe by Elaine Park
2 ounces watermelon juice
2 ounces Champagne
1 ounce St. Germain

They say "simpler is better," but then again they also say "you are what you eat," and unless I didn't get the cannibal memo, that's clearly not true, so they are fucking idiots. Either way, you decide, 'cause the Andrade is fucking easy and delicious. Add everything to a mixing glass with a shitload of ice, stir until you feel it in your pants, about fifteen seconds, and strain into a highball glass. Drink, and wonder if everything they've ever told you is wrong, or if you're just drunk.

Want to just get your buzz on? . . . . *Turn to page 41.*

Attempt to fuck up the un-fuck-up-able with a fucking MF Special

Recipe by Simon Factor

2 ounces sweet vermouth
1 ounce gin
Lemon twist

If you can pour yourself a glass of water, you are overqualified to make this fucking drink. Add the fucking sweet vermouth and gin to a rocks glass with plenty of ice. Stir that shit up until proper cold, then show everyone just exactly how fancy you are by garnishing with a twist of lemon.

Fucked that one up? . . . . *Turn to page 75.*

Make an Italian vagina joke with a fucking

Basil Flower

Recipe by Chelsea Houser

3 ounces gin
1½ ounces St. Germain
½ ounce lime juice
Dash of Demerara sugar
4 basil leaves

O kay, I get it. We've been having a lot of fun at the expense of many a fucking European. But it's not my fault that debt crises, back hair, and who can forget good old fashioned ass fucking are such comedy gold. Well, here is our apology, Europe. In a fucking shaker, muddle the basil with the fucking sugar and lime juice. Add the gin, St. Germain, and some fucking ice, then shake like you're not fucking around. Strain into a chilled cocktail glass, and garnish with a fucking sprig of basil, then drink far too many, and find a European to thank.

Want something
that will make your father
respect you? .... *Turn to page 39.*

Use a flag as a shirt with a fucking Coquito

Recipe by Sara Lugo

2 ounces white rum
2 ounces sweetened condensed milk
2 ounces evaporated milk
2 ounces crema de coco
Dash of vanilla extract
Pinch of cinnamon
Pinch of nutmeg

Coquito is Puerto Rican eggnog, so it's just like regular eggnog, except it drives through my neighborhood with its windows down and music on far too loud. In a Collins glass filled with ice, combine all of that shit and stir until *frio* as fuck. Then drink a few too many, and wonder if a flag can make effective pants, which brings up the issue of: Where are your pants?

Have an aversion to Spanglish? . . . . *Turn to page 115.*

Talk less clearly with a fucking Kentucky Russian

Recipe by James Barker
2 ounces bourbon
1 ounce coffee liqueur
1 ounce half and half

Kentucky and Russia don't have much in common, with the exception being that I can't understand a word either of them fucking says. So it seems fitting that after a few Kentucky Russians nobody will be able to understand you, either. Combine all of that shit in a fucking mixing glass with a shitload of ice. Stir it up until it's colder than one of those mean girls on one of those shows about mean girls or something, or about fifteen seconds. Fucking enjoy.

Don't fucking like that? . . . . *Turn to page 73.*